This book belongs to

What is fair?

Zabed Mohammad, PhD.
Educator & Researcher
Canada

Edited by
Robert Hart

Editorial Assistants
Fatema Yeasmin

Zarir Shiddike

As a little child, I felt sad if someone did
not like me. Was that fair?
But my parents would always love me.
So that was fair!

This is my toy,
but someone wants to play with it.
Is that fair?
My parents gifted me this toy,
and I like to share it with
everybody. So that is fair!

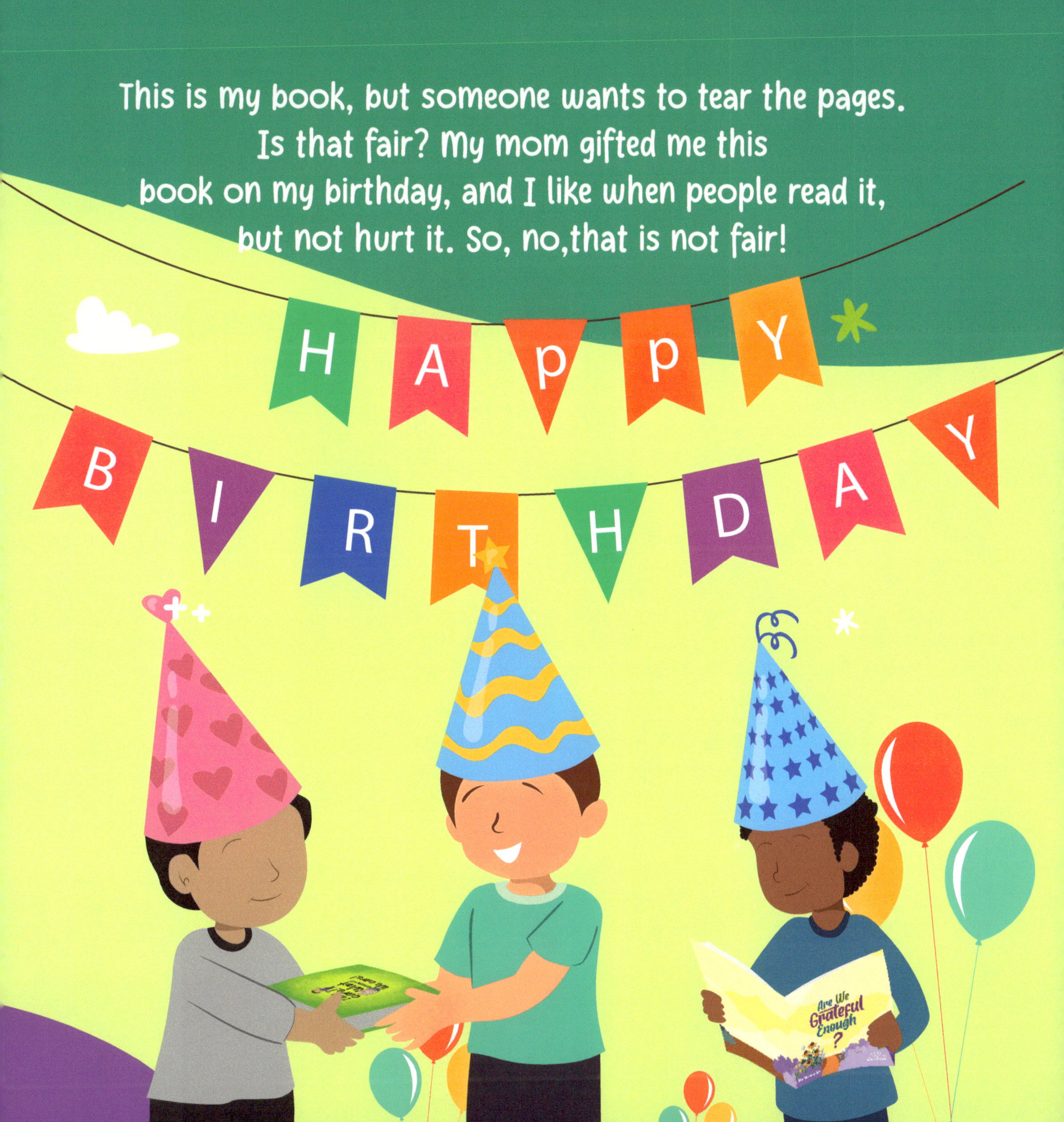

This is my book, but someone wants to tear the pages.
Is that fair? My mom gifted me this
book on my birthday, and I like when people read it,
but not hurt it. So, no,that is not fair!

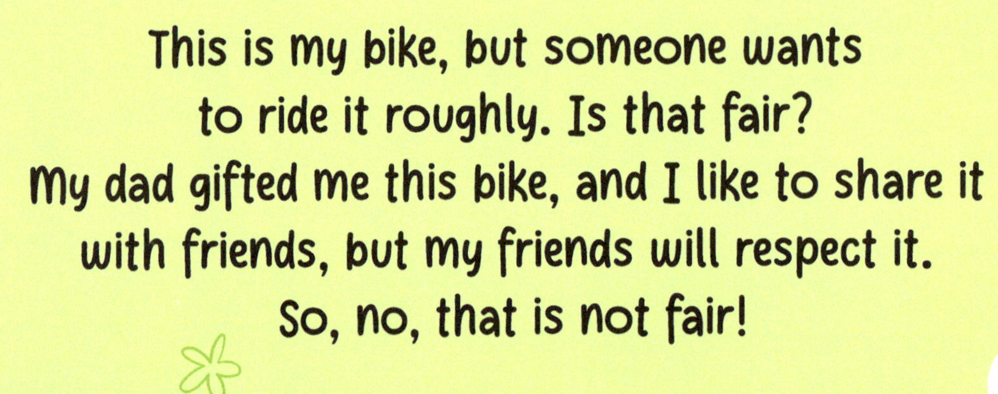

This is my bike, but someone wants
to ride it roughly. Is that fair?
My dad gifted me this bike, and I like to share it
with friends, but my friends will respect it.
So, no, that is not fair!

This is a playground, but someone is blocking the slide, keeping others from enjoying it. Is that fair?
The slide is for everyone, and everyone should be able to play on it.
So, no, that is not fair!

This is the neighbours' ball, and they may not know where it is. Is that fair?
I should return the ball to our neighbours.
That is fair!

This is a sidewalk we all walk on,
but someone has blocked it.
Is that fair?
A sidewalk is for everybody to walk on.
So, no, that is not fair!

Someone has torn the leaves from the
trees, leaving the branches bare.
Is that fair?
Trees give us shade, fruit,
and oxygen for us to breathe.
So, no, that is not fair!

My mom is always asking me to read, write, and do math. Is that fair?
But mom knows how important it is to learn. Hmm.
So, yes, that is fair!

Mom says I have to finish my homework.
Is that fair?
To do well in school, though,
we need to do our homework.
So, yes, that is fair!

Mom says I cannot watch TV or play on
the computer for a long time.
Is that fair?
But she knows that too much screen
time will make me dull and lazy.
So, yes, that is fair!

My mom asks me to help
with house chores.
Is that fair?
But my dad says that home
responsibility starts from
childhood.
So, yes, that is fair!

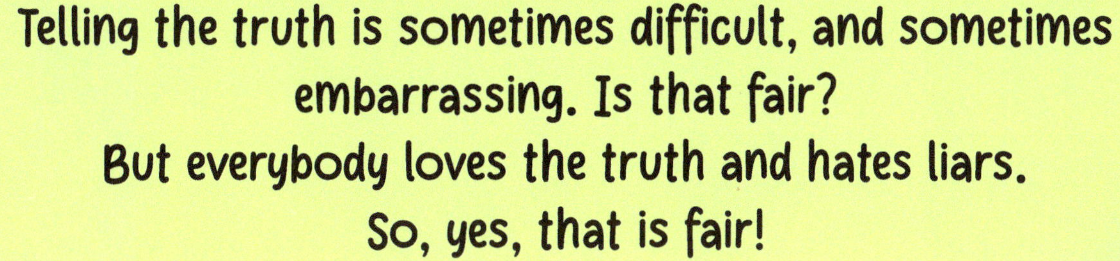

Telling the truth is sometimes difficult, and sometimes embarrassing. Is that fair?
But everybody loves the truth and hates liars.
So, yes, that is fair!

Why must we respect everyone,
regardless of age? Is that fair?
But it is important for all people to feel
respected. So, yes, that is fair!

Having to listen to everyone at home is hard.
Is that fair?
But mom and dad said that listening is a sign of respect.
So, yes, that is fair!

Mom and dad said that I should not fight
or quarrel with my siblings.
Is that fair?
But to have my siblings' respect and care, I must also
respect and care for them. So, yes, that is fair!

Mom and dad said not to play during study time.
Is that fair?
Playing is good for your health, but it should be during our spare
time, not our study time. So, yes, that is fair!

My parents don't always buy
me what I want.
Is that fair?
They say it's because it is important to
be careful with money. Hmm. Okay,

Mom and dad won't let me have a
monkey for a pet. Is that fair?
They say that monkeys are too much
responsibility. That is fair, I guess!

My parents say we can't stay up too late.
Is that fair?
They say it is because we must be careful to get enough sleep in order to stay awake in class. Okay, that is fair!

My parents don't always let me have fast food.
Is that fair?
They say it is because fast food is not healthy and so we should only have it sometimes. All right, that is fair!

We are kids, and some people ignore us
like we are not important.
Is that fair?
But we are the promise of the future,
those who will maintain and improve
our society. So, no, that is not fair!

Mom and dad say that we should be grateful and bow our heads to God in thanks. Is that fair?
They say it is important because God is our creator. So that is fair!

So, what is fair? Hmm.
Is it fair that God created us, giving us the power to improve ourselves and the world? Is it fair that God has promised us a paradise where we can live happily forever?
That is definitely fair! It is fair for every child, and for every living thing!

SOME OF OUR BELOVED BOOKS

1. I am searching! Wait a Minute!
   We are searching too!
2. Are we grateful enough?
3. We may look different!
4. Greetings:
   what are they good for?
5. I love... positive affirmations
   for children
6. I don't care! Wait a moment!
   We care!
7. Work Hard, dream big
8. Manners help
   the world go round!
9. Confidence means power
10. Learning is wonderful

E-mail us for any queries
INFO@KIDSEDUCARE.CA
ZABEDM@KIDSEDUCARE.CA

Copyright © 2022 by Zabed Mohammad,
All rights reserved
CANADA.
Library of Congress Cataloging-in-publication Data
ISBN: 978-1-998923-02-1

Publisher: Kids Edu Care Inc.
Children's Dedicated Learning Series
Website: www.kidseducare.ca
Illustration Copyright © 2022 by
Kids Edu Care Inc.

Illustration & Design
Bee Digital